Mary, Martha and Lazarus

Story by Penny Frank
Illustrated by John Haysom

THE LION STORY BIBLE

44

OXFORD · BATAVIA · SYDNEY

The Bible tells us
how God sent his Son Jesus to show
us what God is like and how we can
belong to God's kingdom.

This story happened in a village
called Bethany, near Jerusalem.
Through his friend Lazarus, Jesus
showed that he was in charge of life
and death.

You can find this story in your
own Bible, in John's Gospel,
chapter 11.

Copyright © 1987 Lion Publishing

Published by
Lion Publishing plc
Sandy Lane West, Oxford, England
ISBN 0 85648 769 4
ISBN 0 7459 1789 5 (paperback)
Lion Publishing
1705 Hubbard Avenue, Batavia, Illinois 60510, USA
ISBN 0 85648 769 4
Albatross Books Pty Ltd
PO Box 320, Sutherland, NSW 2232, Australia
ISBN 0 86760 554 5
ISBN 0 7324 0109 7 (paperback)

First edition 1986, reprinted 1987, 1988, 1990
Paperback edition 1989
Reprinted 1992, 1993

British Library Cataloguing in Publication Data

Frank, Penny
 Mary, Martha and Lazarus. – (The
 Lion Story Bible; 44)
 1. Lazarus – Juvenile literature
 2. Martha, of Bethany – Juvenile
 literature 3. Mary, of Bethany –
 Juvenile literature
 I. Title II. Haysom, John
 226'.59822 BS2344

 ISBN 0-85648-769-4
 ISBN 0-7459-1789-5 (paperback)

Printed and bound in Slovenia

Library of Congress Cataloging in Publication Data

Frank, Penny.
 Mary, Martha and Lazarus.
 (The Lion Story Bible; 44)
 1. Lazarus, of Bethany, Saint – Juvenile
 literature. 2. Mary, of Bethany, Saint –
 Juvenile literature. 3. Martha, Saint –
 Juvenile literature. 4. Bible. N.T. –
 Biography – Juvenile literature. 5. Bible
 stories, English – N.T. John. [1. Lazarus,
 of Bethany, Saint. 2. Mary, of Bethany,
 Saint. 3. Martha, Saint. 4. Bible
 stories – N.T.] I. Haysom, John, ill.
 II. Title. III. Series: Frank, Penny.
 Lion Story Bible; 44.
 BS2640.L3F73 1987 266'.509505
 86-18521
 ISBN 0-85648-769-4
 ISBN 0-7459-1789-5 (paperback)

Mary and Martha were sisters. They
lived in a little house in Bethany, with
their brother Lazarus.

Jesus often came to visit them,
because they were his friends.

One day, in the house in Bethany, everyone was anxious. Lazarus was ill.

It wasn't the kind of illness where people tell you to 'go back to sleep and you'll feel better'. It was the kind where they knew that unless a miracle happened, Lazarus would die.

Mary and Martha had often seen Jesus work miracles. They had seen him make lame people walk and blind people see.

So they sent a message to Jesus to tell him how ill Lazarus was.

5

When Jesus was given the message, his friends were all with him. They knew how much Jesus loved the little family in Bethany. They expected Jesus to set off at once to see Lazarus.

But Jesus just carried on with what he was doing.

'We don't understand,' said one of the disciples to Jesus. 'The message said that Lazarus was so ill, he might die. Why don't you go to heal him?'

'There is a very good reason,' Jesus said. 'Wait and see.'

When they had waited for two days, Jesus said, 'Now it is time to go to Bethany.'

They said 'Goodbye' to the people they had been staying with, and they set off over the hills to Bethany.

As they walked along the street of the
little village the people came out of their
houses to talk to them.

They all knew Jesus.

   'Why didn't you come?' they asked.
'Lazarus is dead.'

Then they all saw Martha, hurrying
down the road towards them.

'Oh Jesus,' she cried. 'You loved him so
much. I'm sure he would not have died
if you had come before.'

Jesus told Martha, 'God will give Lazarus a new life if you believe what I say.'

'I know he will in the end, when we all see God,' Martha said, puzzled.

Jesus said, 'I am the resurrection and the life. Everyone who believes in me has that new life already, even though he dies. Don't be sad, Martha, just believe me.'

When Mary came out of the house, they all went to the cave in the hillside where Lazarus had been buried. The opening of the cave had been closed with a huge stone.

Everyone was crying. They were thinking how much they were going to miss Lazarus. Jesus cried with them.

Then he spoke in a loud voice that made them jump.

'Move that stone away from the cave,' he told them.

'But Lazarus has been dead for four days,' Martha protested.

The stone was pushed away. Jesus looked up and said to God, 'Father, thank you. I know you will do what I ask. And then all these people will believe that you sent me.'

Then Jesus looked at the dark entrance of the cave and shouted, 'Lazarus, come out!'

The people could hardly bear to look.
They were scared.

Mary and Martha trusted Jesus. They
remembered Jesus had said that he was
the resurrection and the life.

Suddenly, Lazarus was standing at the opening of the cave.

The people stood absolutely still, with their mouths wide open. They were amazed.

'Hurry up and untie the grave clothes he's wearing,' Jesus said.

One or two of the braver people did as Jesus said.

Then everyone crowded around Lazarus.
He looked completely well. His skin was
warm and his face was very happy.

Many of the people went back with Jesus to the home of Lazarus, to celebrate. Martha and Mary were so glad that Jesus had come.

Some of the people went away to the city. They told everyone they met about what had happened.

'It was amazing,' they said. 'When Jesus called him, Lazarus came out of the cave, and now he is alive and well.'

But the priests and rulers were not pleased. They were more jealous of Jesus than ever before.

The Lion Story Bible is made up of 52 individual stories for young readers, building up an understanding of the Bible as one story — God's story — a story for all time and all people.

The New Testament section (numbers 31–52) covers the life and teaching of God's Son, Jesus. The stories are about the people he met, what he did and what he said. Almost all we know about the life of Jesus is recorded in the four Gospels — Matthew, Mark, Luke and John. The word gospel means 'good news'.

The last four stories in this section are about the first Christians, who started to tell others the 'good news', as Jesus had commanded them — a story which continues today all over the world.

The story of *Mary, Martha and Lazarus* comes from the New Testament, John's Gospel, chapter 11. There is more about these friends of Jesus in Luke's Gospel, chapter 10, verses 38–42.

When Jesus performed what we call 'miracles', suspending the normal, natural laws, it was not just to impress, or to answer a need. His miracles were signs intended to show people that he was the one he claimed to be.

When he said, 'I am the resurrection and the life,' and actually brought Lazarus to life again, people knew that what he said was really true. He had power over life and death. And soon, in his own death and resurrection he would defeat death for ever. Now, those who love him need not be afraid of dying. It is not the end, but the beginning of a new and better life.

The next book in the series, number 45: *People Jesus met*, tells the stories of a number of people who never forgot the day they met Jesus.